My First Book about

Pandas

Children's Picture Books

by Annalee Davidson

Mendon Cottage Books

JD-Biz Publishing

Read More Amazing Animal Books

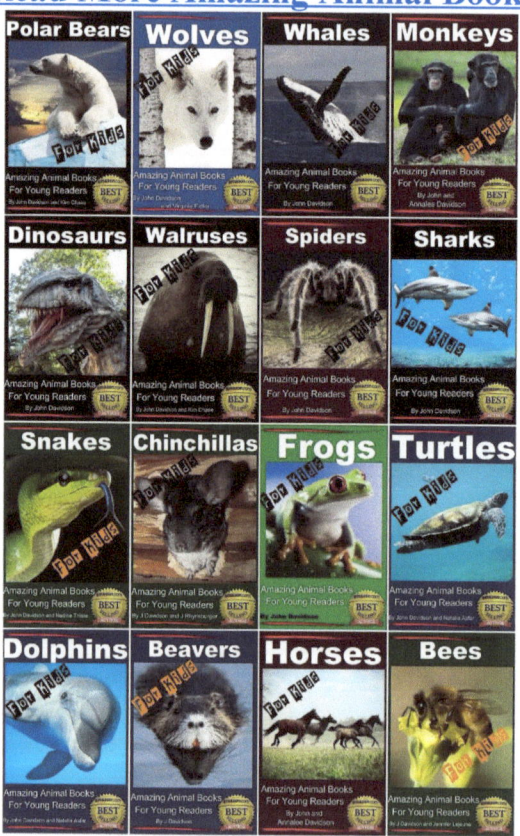

Purchase at Amazon.com
Download Free Books!
http://MendonCottageBooks.com

Table of Contents

1. 10 Facts About Pandas

The following are ten facts about pandas:

1. The Panda has 5 fingers and a thumb.

2. There are less than 10 million pandas in the world.

3. Pandas are found mostly in the mountains of China.

4. Pandas inhabit mostly mountain forests, which are filled with trees and bamboo.

5. Giant Pandas spend 15 hours each day eating, mostly on bamboo.

6. Giant pandas are one of the few bear types that don't like to hide.

7. Pandas live at high altitudes of about 1,500 to 3,000M.

8. They have thick and oily fur that keeps them warm.

9. Pandas like to live alone.

10. When they are born a baby panda is about 1/900th the mother's body size.

2. What Are Panda Bears?

It's the world's most famous bear!

They are found in China, and even though this big bear's eyesight isn't the best, it has a great sense of smell that it uses to find what it is looking for.

3. Types of Pandas

Types of panda :

The two different types of Pandas are the Giant and the Lesser panda.

Giant panda :

Giant Pandas are 2-3 ft tall on all fours and like to eat bamboo. It is also known as the black & white panda. This is the most common type of Panda

Lesser Panda :

The lesser panda looks more like a fox because of its red colored fur and small size.

Red pandas live high up in the trees and sleeps during the daytime.

4. Pandas Are Endangered

A Panda is one of the world's most popular endangered animals.

Hunting is a big threat to their survival.

Since there are less pandas in the wild, it makes it harder for them to grow as a species. Less baby pandas means less Pandas overall.

5. Panda Bears Habitat

Pandas thick fur keeps them warm from the cold and helps them blend in with the trees and grass around them.

Panda bears are great climbers and love to climb on trees and rocks.

6. Where Do Pandas Live

Pandas live in Mountainous areas that have lots of bamboo. These places are also called bamboo forests.

7. What Do Panda Bears Eat

A panda's main food choice is bamboo, but they do sometimes eat fruits and berries.

Because bamboo has such little amounts of nutrients in it, Pandas have to eat lots of it to have enough energy for the day.

8. Giant Panda Bear Behavior

The giant panda bear usually lives by itself and likes to do things in the cooler morning and evenings.

They also like to spend most of their time sleeping and eating.

9. What do Giant Panda Bears Look Like

1. Male Pandas can measure up to 6 feet long.

2. Pandas can weigh up to 350 pounds.

3. Their body is covered by a thick fur that keeps them warm and protects them from the weather.

5. Special eyes help pandas see well in the dark, but not so well in the daytime.

6. They have the biggest molars of any land mammal.

7. They have a big black band across their shoulders and legs.

10. Giant Panda Bear Predators

Here are some well known predators of the panda

Jackals: They hunt pandas for food.

Leopards: They can run very fast and can catch pandas easily.

 Yellow-throated martens: These mostly prey on baby pandas.

Lesser Panda

Read More Amazing Animal Books

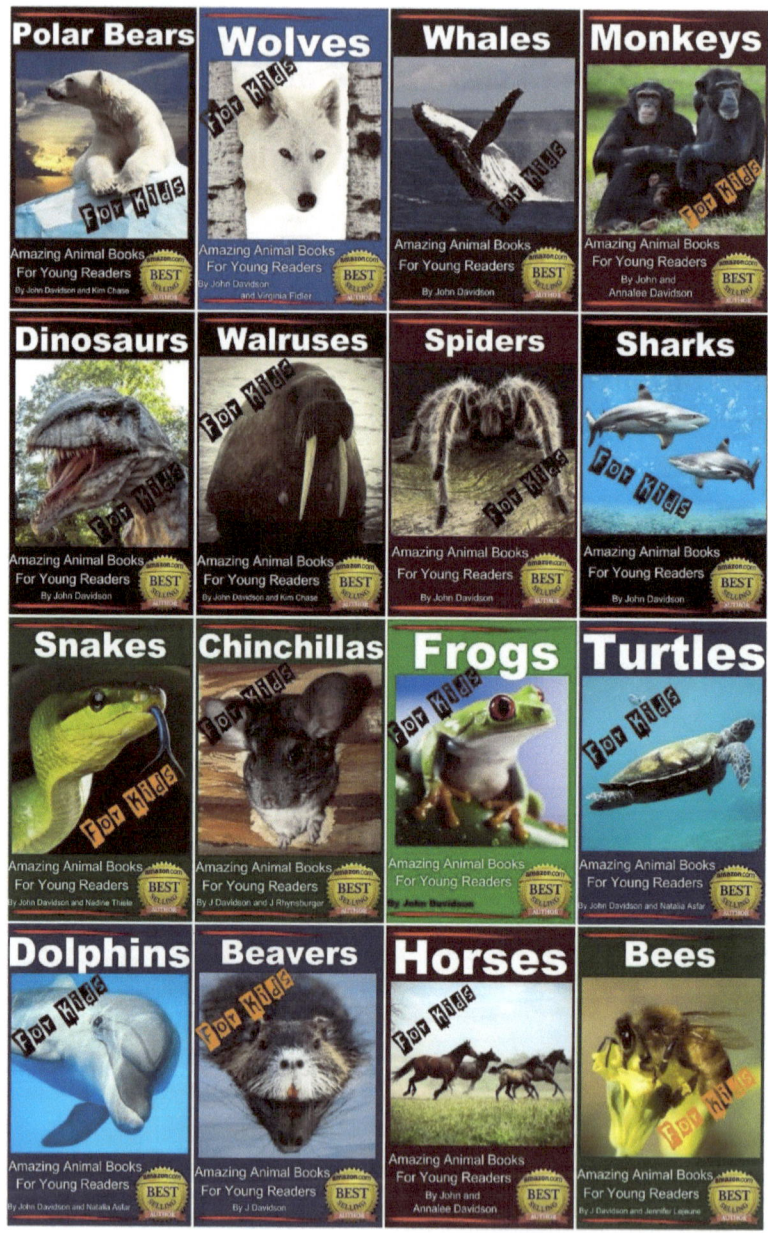

Purchase at Amazon.com

Website http://AmazingAnimalBooks.com

Horses
For Kids

Amazing Animal Books
For Young Readers
By John and
Annalee Davidson

Ponies
For Kids

Meadow Cottage Books

AmazingAnimalBooks
For Young Readers
Rachel Smith

Ten Amazing Horses
For Kids

Nature Books for Kids
JD-Biz Publishing
K. Bennett

Akhal-Teke
"The Golden Horse
of the desert"
For Kids

Nature Books for Kids
JD-Biz Publishing
K. Bennett

Suffolk-Punch
"The Gentle Giant"
For Kids

Nature Books for Kids
JD-Biz Publishing
K. Bennett

Shires
"The great Horse"
For Kids

Nature Books for Kids
JD-Biz Publishing
K. Bennett

Colonial Spanish
"Horse of the Americas"
For Kids

Nature Books for Kids
JD-Biz Publishing
K. Bennett

Canadian
"The Little Iron Horse"
For Kids

Nature Books for Kids
JD-Biz Publishing
K. Bennett

Cleveland Bays
"History and Future"
Horses For Kids

Nature Books for Kids
JD-Biz Publishing
K. Bennett

Top Ten Dog Breeds For Kids

Amazing Animal Books For Young Readers

Kisha Bennett & John Davidson

German Shepherds

Dog Books for Kids

K. Bennett

Bulldogs

Dog Books for Kids

K. Bennett

Dachshund

Dog Books for Kids

K. Bennett

Poodles

Dog Books for Kids

K. Bennett

Labrador Retrievers

Dog Books for Kids

K. Bennett

Rottweilers

Dog Books for Kids

K. Bennett

Boxers

Dog Books for Kids

K. Bennett

Golden Retrievers

Dog Books for Kids

K. Bennett

Puppies

Dog Books For Kids

Amazing Animal Books

By John Davidson

Beagles

Dog Books for Kids

K. Bennett

Yorkshire Terriers

Dog Books for Kids

K. Bennett

Dogs

Top Ten Dog Breeds For Kids

Amazing Animal Books For Young Readers

Zahra Jazeel & John Davidson

Cats For Kids

Amazing Animal Books For Young Readers

K. Bennett & John Davidson

Foxes For Kids

Amazing Animal Books For Young Readers

Zahra Jazeel & John Davidson

Wolves For Kids

Amazing Animal Books For Young Readers

By John Davidson and Virginia Fidler

Our books are available at

1. Amazon.com
2. Barnes and Noble
3. Itunes
4. Kobo
5. Smashwords
6. Google Play Books

Download Free Books!
http://MendonCottageBooks.com

Publisher

JD-Biz Corp

P O Box 374

Mendon, Utah 84325

http://www.jd-biz.com/